Darlington
TROLLEYBUSES

Stephen Lockwood
Series editor Robert J Harley

Middleton Press

Cover photographs

Front cover
Typical of the later years of Darlington's trolleybuses were the boxy centre-entrance utility Karriers, such as no 20, seen here in this rare colour view on leafy Woodland Road. This particular vehicle survived, rebuilt as a modern double decker with front entrance and heaters, in service with Bradford City Transport until July 1971. It is now kept in working order as an exhibit in the Trolleybus Museum at Sandtoft. Photobus / J Copland

Rear cover
Tramcar 15 is seen at Eastbourne terminus during the First World War. Further details of this view are contained in the caption to photograph 95.

Published May 2004

ISBN 1 904474 33 0

© Middleton Press, 2004

Design   Deborah Esher
              David Pede

Published by
              Middleton Press
              Easebourne Lane
              Midhurst, West Sussex
              GU29 9AZ
Tel: 01730 813169
Fax: 01730 812601
Email: info@middletonpress.co.uk
www.middletonpress.co.uk

Printed & bound by MPG Books Ltd, Bodmin, Cornwall

CONTENTS

INTRODUCTION AND ACKNOWLEDGEMENTS

On Ist June 1904, the electric tramway system in Darlington was opened, heralding a new era of municipal enterprise in the town. The network was converted to trolleybus operation in 1926, and this, improved and extended, lasted until July 1957 when the last electric vehicles were replaced by motorbuses. The publication of this book is to commemorate the centenary of the opening of electric street transport in Darlington.

Darlington achieved great fame as a railway town. The Stockton and Darlington Railway, the 'world's first public railway', was established in 1825, being financed by Darlington businessmen. The town's trams and trolleybuses also had claims to fame – the first municipal electric tramway system to be authorised under the 1896 Light Railways Act and, apart from a short-lived experimental motorbus service using hired vehicles in the late-1920s, one of only two municipal transport undertakings to rely entirely on electric traction until 1950 (the other being Ipswich). The tramcars proudly bore the legend 'Darlington Corporation Light Railways' on their sides rather than the more usual 'Corporation Tramways'. The system was not large, with 24 trams serving 4.87 miles/7.8 km of route, although by 1949 the trolleybuses had grown to a maximum of 66 vehicles running over 12.35 miles/19.9 km, well in excess of the route mileage of the trams.

Readers of my previous volumes for Middleton Press, ('Huddersfield Trolleybuses' and 'Bradford Trolleybuses'), will know that my interest in these vehicles began at an early age in my home town of Huddersfield. As I gained knowledge of other trolleybus systems around the country, that at Darlington stood out, because the system and vehicles seemed the very antithesis of that of my home town. Darlington ran 33-seat single-deckers with central entrance rather than 70-seat three axle double-deckers. The routes were short – a maximum of two miles from the Market Place compared with the five miles and more of some Huddersfield routes. My interest was whetted by a school friend who had relatives in Darlington and visited regularly, describing the vehicles and routes he had seen. It is a matter of regret to me that I was never able to see these little single deckers with their extra long trolley booms, the passengers sitting facing each other inside, and the draughty open centre doorway. Nor was I able, during the last summer of the Park Lane route, to watch one reverse across the road end at the terminus as the 'Elizabethan' express, non-stop to Edinburgh, thundered across the adjacent railway bridge.

The rebuilt ex-Darlington trolleybuses that operated in Bradford with their GHN and LHN registration letters until 1971 were well known to me. I rode on the very last to operate, LHN 834, when it was the final trolleybus on Bradford's Clayton route. However, fate took a hand and in 1976 I was appointed as Traffic Officer with Darlington Borough Transport, and the town has been my home ever since. On my desk, there were two reminders of the electric traction era; a large sheet of plate glass which originated from the rear window of a late-1930s streamlined trolleybus and a curiously shaped paperweight. This was formed from the upper part of a trolley head, complete with carbon insert. An inscription

3

on the wooden base read 'Slipper from the last Darlington trolleybus, 31st July 1957'.

Today, the streets of Darlington are largely unchanged from when trams and trolleybuses ran, and apart from the area affected by the inner ring road constructed during the 1960s and 1970s, most of the locations depicted in this book are recognisable today. Of the trams, the last evidence was some rails, 3 feet 6 inches/1067mm apart, lining the pits in the former tram depot at Haughton Road. This was demolished in the late 1990s following the untimely demise of the Council-owned Darlington Transport Company in November 1994. Reminders of the trolleybuses can still be seen at the Lingfield Lane end of Yarm Road, where four former traction poles still survive carrying street lighting, the 'leaning back' attitude indicating their original role of supporting the trolley wires. At the former Coniscliffe Road terminus, the set-back kerb-line opposite the junction with Baydale Road is still intact. This assisted trolleybus drivers to negotiate the tight turning circle at this point.

This book is not a definitive history of the trams or trolleybuses – that work has still to be written, but it does give a flavour of Darlington's electric street transport that is still fondly remembered by many residents. Previous works on the subject which have been consulted for this volume are two excellent magazine articles; G S Hearse : 'The Tramways of Darlington' in a 1953 Tramway Review and JS King : 'Darlington Trolleybuses' in Buses magazine, July 1968. In addition there is Ian Wood's useful general history of Darlington Transport published in 1996. The pictorial content follows a geographical journey around the town, route by route, followed by a review of the town centre area and rolling stock. The supply of photographs depicting the system has proved to be extremely limited, and although several transport photographers did make visits to the town to record these vehicles there do not appear to have been any local residents who routinely photographed the trams and trolleybuses. This paucity has resulted in a very small minority of views in the book, which show key facets of the system, having to be reproduced from poor quality images, including newspaper archives and I hope readers will make an allowance for this.

My thanks go to all the photographers whose work appears here and I am also grateful to the following for so willingly responding to my requests for information and the loan of material for this project; Stanley King, Roy Marshall, Philip Battersby, Peter Cardno, Don Jones of the London Trolleybus Preservation Society, John Watson, Bob Kell, David Packer, Eric Old, Roy Brook, John Fozard, David Smithies, Robert Harley, Douglas Parker, Colin Routh, Alan Cross, Arnold Richardson of Photobus, Gordon Coates, George Flynn, Dewi Williams, Mrs Marion Turner, Cliff at C&G Model Railways, Chris Lloyd (Assistant Editor of The Northern Echo), and the staffs of the Darlington Centre for Local Studies and The National Tramway Museum Library. My gratitude goes to Stanley King, Philip Battersby, Peter Cardno and Philip Jenkinson for reading through the text and suggesting additions and improvements and to Gordon Coates and Paul Watson for excellent photographic printing work. The magnificent map of the trolleybus wiring has been drawn specially by John Gillham, and I am greatly indebted to him for the opportunity to enhance the book by its inclusion. In addition, John has revised the tramway map, provided several photographs and made useful comments on my text.

Finally, thanks are due to my wife Eileen, who, as always, has supported me in the preparation of this book. She has the advantage of me as she actually grew up in the days when Darlington had a silent, fume free trolleybus system.

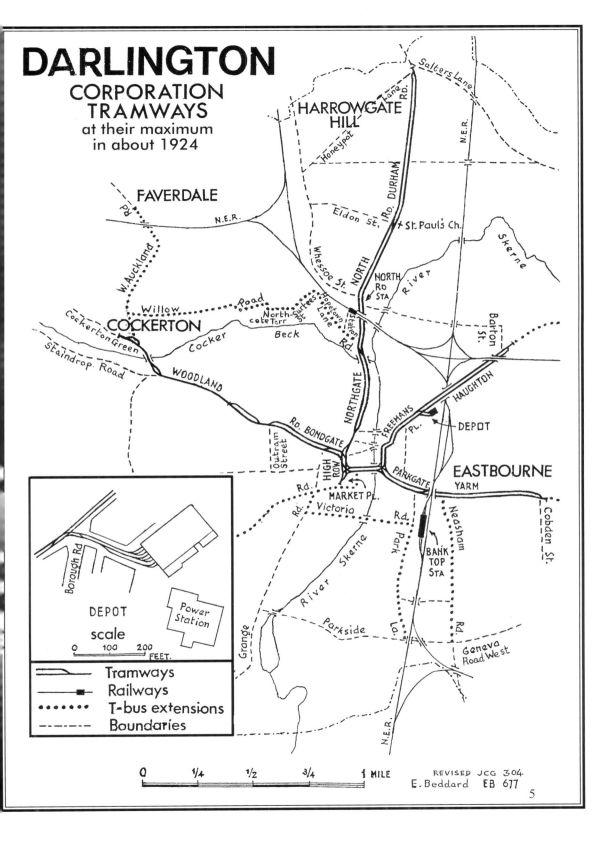

DARLINGTON
CORPORATION
TRAMWAYS
at their maximum
in about 1924

FAVERDALE

HARROWGATE HILL

Honeypot Lane

Salters Lane

N.E.R.

Rd.

W. Auckland

N.E.R.

Eldon St.

RD. DURHAM

Rd.

NORTH

+ St. Paul's Ch.

Whessoe St.

NORTH RD STA

Skerne

River

Willow Road

Cockerton Green

COCKERTON

Northcote Terr.

Surtees St.

Hopetown Lane

Station Rd.

Barton St.

Cocker

Beck

Staindrop Road

WOODLAND

NORTHGATE

HAUGHTON

DEPOT

Rd. BONDGATE

Outram Street

FREEMANS PL.

EASTBOURNE

HIGH ROW

PARKGATE

YARM

Rd.

MARKET PL.

Victoria

Rd.

Park Rd.

Neasham

Cobden St.

BANK TOP STA

Grange

River Skerne

Parkside

La.

Rd.

Geneva Road West

N.E.R.

Borough Rd

DEPOT

Power Station

scale

0   100   200
FEET.

⎯⎯⎯ Tramways
■■■ Railways
•••••• T-bus extensions
— — — Boundaries

0   ¼   ½   ¾   1 MILE

REVISED JCG 304
E. Beddard   EB 677

5

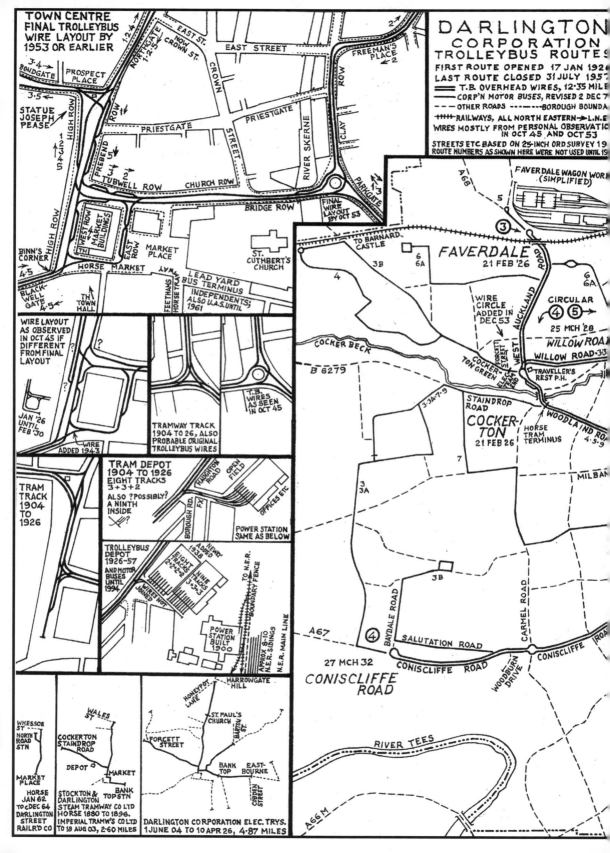

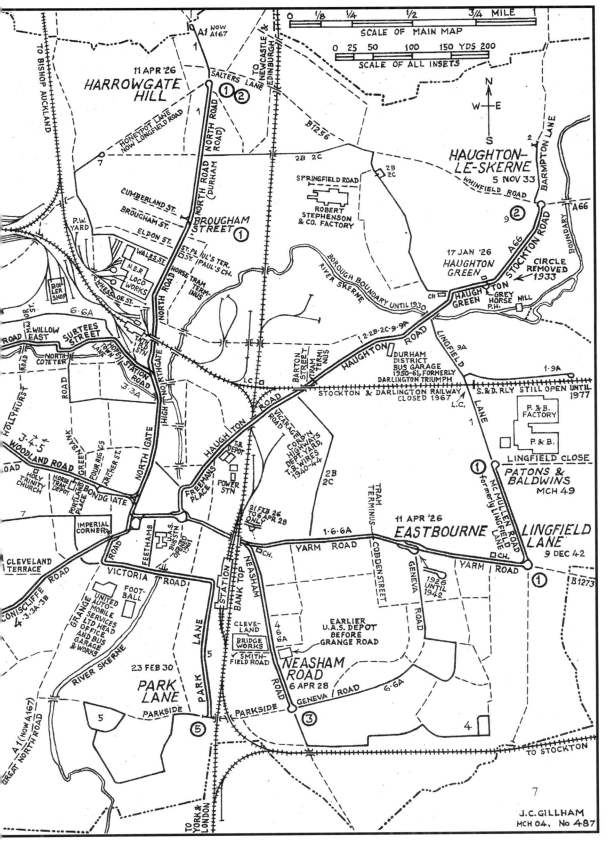

SCALE OF MAIN MAP
⅛ ¼ ½ ¾ MILE 1

SCALE OF ALL INSETS
0 25 50 100 150 YDS 200

A1 NOW A167
TO NEWCASTLE & EDINBURGH

11 APR '26
HARROWGATE HILL
①②
SALTERS LANE

TO BISHOP AUCKLAND

HONEYPOT LANE
NOW LONGFIELD ROAD

B1256

HAUGHTON-LE-SKERNE
5 NOV 33

BARMPTON LANE

WHINFIELD ROAD

A66

CUMBERLAND ST.
BROUGHAM ST.
ELDON ST.

BROUGHAM STREET ①

SPRINGFIELD ROAD
ROBERT STEPHENSON & CO. FACTORY

2B 2C
2B 2C

⑨②
A66
A66 STOCKTON ROAD
BOUNDARY

17 JAN '26
HAUGHTON GREEN

CIRCLE REMOVED 1933

P.W. YARD
WALES ST.
N.E.R. LOCO WORKS
WHESSOE ST.
ST. PAUL'S TER.
ST. PAUL'S CH.
HORSE TRAM TERMINUS

NORTH ROAD (DURHAM ROAD)
NORTH ROAD

RIVER SKERNE
BOROUGH BOUNDARY UNTIL 1930

CH.
HAUGHTON GREEN
GREY HORSE P.H.
HILL

BOILER SHOP
6·6A
ROAD EAST
WILLOW ROAD
SURTEES STREET
NORTH COTE TER.
3·3A
ROAD
HOLLYHURST

STATION ROAD
HIGH NORTHGATE NORTHGATE

2·2B·2C·9·9A
HAUGHTON ROAD

LINGFIELD ROAD
9A

DURHAM DISTRICT BUS GARAGE 1950-61, FORMERLY DARLINGTON TRIUMPH

1·9A

S.&D. RLY STILL OPEN UNTIL 1977

BARTON STREET TRAM TERMINUS

STOCKTON & DARLINGTON RAILWAY CLOSED 1967
L.C.

LANE

P. & B. FACTORY
P. & B.

HAUGHTON ROAD

VICARAGE ROAD
CORPN HIGHWAYS DEPT YARD, T-B. WIRES 1940-44

2B 2C

LINGFIELD CLOSE

3·4·5
WOODLAND ROAD
HOLY TRINITY CHURCH
HORSE TRAM DEPOT
GREENBANK ROAD
FOUR RIGGS
ARCHER ST.

NORTHGATE

T.B. DEPOT
POWER STN
FREEMANS PLACE

21 FEB 26 TO 6 APR 28 ONLY

①
PATONS & BALDWINS
MCH 49

MC MULLEN ROAD formerly LINGFIELD LANE

IMPERIAL CORNER

7
CLEVELAND TERRACE

U.A.S. BUS STN OPENED 1961

FEETHAMS

VICTORIA ROAD

FOOTBALL

GRANGE ROAD
UNITED AUTOMOBILE SERVICES LTD HEAD OFFICE AND BUS GARAGE & WORKS

11 APR '26
EASTBOURNE

TRAM TERMINUS
COBDEN STREET

1·6·6A
YARM ROAD

GENEVA ROAD
1926 UNTIL 1942

LINGFIELD LANE
9 DEC 42

①
YARM ROAD
B1273
CH.

4·3·3A·3B
CONISCLIFFE ROAD

RIVER SKERNE

PORTLAND PLACE
BONDGATE

STATION
BANK TOP

PARK LANE

NEASHAM ROAD

CLEVELAND BRIDGE WORKS
SMITHFIELD ROAD

4·6A
4·6A

EARLIER U.A.S. DEPOT BEFORE GRANGE ROAD

6·6A

A1 (NOW A167)
GREAT NORTH ROAD

23 FEB 30
PARK LANE

PARK LANE

⑤
PARKSIDE

5

PARKSIDE

NEASHAM ROAD
6 APR 28

GENEVA ROAD

③
GENEVA ROAD

6·6A

4

TO STOCKTON

TO YORK & LONDON

7

J.C.GILLHAM
MCH 04, No 487

GEOGRAPHICAL SETTING

Darlington, situated in the southern-most part of County Durham, lies on the River Skerne, a tributary of the River Tees. The Tees meanders around the south of the town and forms the boundary with North Yorkshire (formerly the North Riding of Yorkshire). The nearest large settlements are Durham to the north (18 miles), Stockton and Middlesbrough to the east (11/15 miles), Northallerton to the south (16 miles) and Bishop Auckland to the north-west (12 miles). The Great North Road (A1) between London and Edinburgh ran through the centre of the town until a bypass was opened in the mid-1960s. Darlington's main tram and trolleybus route followed the A1 as far as Harrowgate Hill, and during the later years of trolleybuses increasing traffic congestion caused operating problems for the Transport Department.

Prior to 1825, Darlington was a market town with a thriving textile industry dominated by the Pease family who were prominent Quakers. Their investment in the Stockton and Darlington Railway and the subsequent opening of main railway routes through Darlington to London and Scotland transformed the town, attracting heavy engineering industries including the locomotive building works of the North Eastern Railway in North Road. The railway caused problems for the tram and trolleybus system in the form of low bridges over most of the main roads. This meant that single-deck vehicles predominated, and the use of double-deckers, desirable due to the amount of passenger traffic, was severely curtailed.

Darlington received its Charter of Incorporation as a Borough in 1867 and achieved County Borough status in 1915. As late as 1930 the Borough Boundary was expanded to include substantial areas to the east of the town. Amongst these were Haughton-le-Skerne and Lingfield, both part of the later trolleybus network. The population at the outbreak of the Second World War was 76,000. Since 1997, Darlington has been designated a unitary authority, administratively separate from County Durham.

HISTORICAL BACKGROUND

Before telling the story of Darlington's electric street transport, it is necessary to mention briefly the two separate horse tramways that preceded the electric era in the town.

The famous American entrepreneur, George Francis Train, opened the first public street tramway in Britain in Birkenhead in 1860. The following year Train opened similar lines in London. In Darlington, the Darlington Street Railroad Company, using Train's patents, constructed a tramway between the Market Place and the Stockton and Darlington Railway Company's station in North Road (now known as Darlington North Road Station). A short branch continued along North Road under the railway bridge as far as the junction with Whessoe Street (now Whessoe Road). The depot was in McNay Street adjacent to the railway station and the directors included members of the Pease family, Train being advisor to the company. Operations started in January 1862 using two cars named 'Nelson' and 'Wellington'. The line suffered the same problems as Train's lines elsewhere, mainly due to difficulties with the step rail which stood proud of the road surface rather than flush with it. This caused damage to other road vehicles as well as injuries to pedestrians and animals. The operation was eventually abandoned about the end of 1864, the exact date being uncertain.

Darlington remained tram-less until 1880, when the Stockton and Darlington Steam Tramway Company established a small system of horse trams running on 3 feet/915mm gauge track (The company ran steam trams in Stockton, hence its title). There were three routes, each starting from the Market Place, these being to Bank Top Station via Feethams and Victoria Road; to Cockerton (Staindrop Road) via Woodland Road and to North Road (Wales Street). The cars, twelve in total, were a mixture of single and double deckers, of which about seven were required to operate the service. The depot was at the Bondgate end of Woodland Road near Portland Place. The Bank Top Station line was abandoned in 1885, but the remaining two routes survived to be taken over in 1896 by the Bristol based Imperial Tramways Company which ran the tramways in Middlesbrough. Imperial Tramways wished to reconstruct and electrify the system, and obtained a provisional Light Railway Order to do this in 1899. Meanwhile, Darlington Corporation had established an electricity power station in 1900 and wished to use its home produced power to run the tram system. Accordingly, in January 1902, Imperial Tramways was paid £7,600 for its operation including the provisional Light Railway Order. Although the Corporation now owned the horse tramway, its operation was leased to the former tramway manager. The full Light Railway Order to electrify and extend the tramway was confirmed in July 1902 and accordingly the last horse tram ran on 18th August 1903. This was to allow complete reconstruction of the track and the provision of overhead wiring and once again Darlington was tram-less.

Darlington's new municipal electric tramway consisted of four routes radiating from the Market Place, these being to Harrowgate Hill (Honeypot Lane - later renamed Longfield Road), Haughton Road (Barton Street), Eastbourne (Cobden Street) and Cockerton (Forcett Street). The area covered by these routes reflected the built-up areas of the town at that time. The track gauge was 3 feet 6 inches. Apart from the Cockerton route, which had single track with passing loops, the system was double track throughout although a short section of single track was necessary in the narrow town centre section of Northgate between Crown Street and Bondgate. Although the overhead was mainly supported by bracket arms, ornate centre poles were provided in Tubwell Row, Bondgate, Parkgate and High Northgate complete with an integral street light. In Woodland Road on the Cockerton route, the poles were planted in the roadway itself with very short bracket arms over the track. The eight-road depot was constructed adjacent to the power station in Haughton Road, mid-way along the Barton Street line. The Electricity Department of the Corporation was under the same management as the tramway department (known as the Light Railways Department) and the new manager was Mr JRP Lunn.

The presence of low railway bridges at North Road, Barton Street and Bank Top Station

resulted in the purchase of sixteen single-deck tramcars seating 28 passengers from GF Milnes and Co. One of these was used for the Board of Trade inspection on 25th May 1904, and the formal opening of the system was planned for the following week.

The municipal electric transport era commenced on 1st June 1904, when a procession of trams set off from High Row, visiting each route in turn. Public service began on the Harrowgate Hill route the following day, and the other services were opened shortly afterwards. Trams ran to a basic ten minute frequency, with the Harrowgate Hill and Eastbourne service linked as a through route, a practice which survived tram, trolleybus and motorbus operation right up to the demise of public ownership in 1994. Cockerton trams ran to Bank Top Station, whilst the Barton Street line shuttled to and from the Market Place. At night colour lights on the front of the cars indicated their routes as follows :- Harrowgate Hill - yellow; Eastbourne or Cockerton – green; Barton Street – purple. The busiest route was the through Harrowgate Hill to Eastbourne service which served the North Road locomotive works and the dense housing and industrial area around Bank Top Station. Extra cars ran between the Market Place and St Paul's Church (just beyond the loco works) at peak hours.

Despite housing and industrial growth away from the tramway, there was no further route development of the system, apart from some re-positioning of crossovers and the lengthening of loops on the Cockerton route. However, the tram fleet was augmented when two handsome double-deck open balcony cars entered service in 1913, although low bridges prevented them from operating on certain parts of the system. Similar restrictions applied to six open-top double-deck cars bought in 1918 from Sheerness in Kent.

By the first half of the 1920s consideration was being given to the future of the trams. Development of the town meant that extensions to public transport provision were required to serve new areas and the existing infrastructure was in dire need of replacement, especially the rails, most of which were worn out. Alfred Baker, the General Manager of Birmingham City Tramways, was called in to advise on the direction the undertaking should take. He had just inaugurated a trolleybus service in Birmingham. In his report dated 22nd March 1924, he highlighted the poor state of the tramway, for instance stating 'in some cases the wheel flanges are running on the bottom of the rail grooves.' He recommended the Corporation to replace its tram system and extend the network using eighteen trolleybuses, taking into account the greater operating speed of this type of vehicle.

Accordingly the Town Clerk was instructed to apply to Parliament for the necessary powers to operate trolley vehicles and omnibuses over an enlarged route system. These were granted under the 'Darlington Corporation (Transport &c Act) 1925'. One restrictive, and far reaching part of this Act was contained in Sections 25 and 26, which prohibited the Corporation from operating services over one mile outside the Borough boundary without the permission of United Automobile Services or the London and North Eastern Railway Company. This would still allow the Haughton Road service to be extended to Haughton–le–Skerne village, which until 1930 was just outside the Borough. These restrictions remained in place until well after the trolleybus era and were not revoked until 1985 (just prior to bus route licensing deregulation) under the Darlington (Revocation of Restriction) Order 1985.

Once again Darlingtonians were subject to a complete change in their public transport, although this time the doomed trams were able to operate whilst trolleybus wiring was erected. The conversion work was carried out by Clough, Smith and Co using span wiring and bracket arm suspension, retaining as many of the tram poles as possible. Twenty box-like single deck, centre entrance 'trolley-omnibuses', which set the design trend for future vehicle deliveries, were ordered from Straker-Clough, the first of these being delivered in late 1925 for driver training purposes. Public trolleybus operation commenced on Sunday 17th January 1926, when the Barton Street trams, having made their last runs the previous evening, were replaced by trolleybuses. These ran beyond the tram terminus into the village of Haughton-le-Skerne, almost a mile from Barton Street and 1/3rd of a mile beyond the Borough boundary at Haughton Bridge. Sunday 21st February saw the

Cockerton to Bank Top Station trams replaced with trolleybuses, the route being extended along West Auckland Road to Faverdale, serving new housing and the new LNER wagon works. As soon as enough vehicles were available, this service was extended from Bank Top along Yarm Road as far as Geneva Road running most of the way alongside the Eastbourne trams. This route linking was a short-term measure until the Neasham Road service opened in 1928. The remaining tram route, the 'main line' between Eastbourne and Harrowgate Hill, was converted on Sunday 11th April. Due to only nineteen of the twenty trolleybuses being available for service, trams did have to turn out at peak hours for a short while after 10th April to maintain services, much to the surprise of early-morning shift workers.

Extensions of the trolleybus system into new areas previously unserved by public transport were now introduced as follows:-

Willow Road circle -
                    Sunday 25th March 1928
Neasham Road - Good Friday 6th April 1928
Park Lane (via Victoria Road) -
                    Sunday 23rd February 1930
Coniscliffe Road (Baydale Road)-
                    Sunday 27th March 1932

Additionally, the Haughton route was extended a further 1/3rd mile to the Gatehouse at Barmpton Lane end from Sunday 5th November 1933. By this time Haughton-le-Skerne had been incorporated into the Borough.

The system was now established, and the pattern of services was

Harrowgate Hill – Eastbourne
Harrowgate Hill – Haughton
Faverdale   – Neasham Road
Coniscliffe Road – Willow Road
                    (anti-clockwise circle)
Park Lane   – Willow Road
                    (clockwise circle)

The fleet increased in size reaching 44 vehicles by 1937, these additions being to the general style of the original Strakers, although by the mid-1930s this was a very old fashioned design. In 1937, the General Manager, Mr Lunn, retired and was replaced by Mr WJH Penman, who became manager of the Transport Department only and not additionally the Electricity undertaking as had previously been the case. Vehicle deliveries for the rest of the decade, and into the first part of the war, were to a very modern and handsome streamlined design.

The war years saw several changes and improvements to the system. Additional turning facilities were erected in the town centre at Bondgate and on North Road at Cumberland Street near the locomotive works, a point always shown on route indicators as 'Brougham Street'. A short route extension opened on Wednesday 9th December 1942 to take the Eastbourne trolleybuses as far as Lingfield Lane serving the residents of a war workers' housing scheme. Female platform staff were employed, eventually including drivers and inspectors. During 1943, the Coniscliffe Road service was experimentally linked with that to Haughton, involving new wiring in the town centre. This work included the installation of the first automatic frog on the system and many more 'automatic switches', as they were termed in Darlington, followed at major wiring junctions. A further consequence of the war was the dispersal of the older vehicles to the Corporation's Highways depot, in case the trolleybus depot was hit by enemy action. The original Straker fleet was largely replaced during the war by 24 trolleybuses built to utility specification with wooden seats.

After the war, the intention of the Corporation Streets Committee to raise the headroom of the North Road and Station bridges prompted the ordering of six double-deck BUT trolleybuses. However, history began to repeat itself, and the continued future of the trolleybus system came under scrutiny. The condition of the wiring, power supply, and the prospect of nationalisation of the municipal power station, together with the need to extend public transport services into new housing estates, prompted the Council to approve a policy of replacement of trolleybuses by motorbuses. The Ministry of Transport urged caution, as changes in the ownership of all bus undertakings in the north-east region were being proposed, and the Council put its trolleybus replacement plan on hold. One further trolleybus development, marking the pinnacle of the system's development, was the opening in March 1949 of a half-mile extension of the Eastbourne route along McMullen Road to serve the newly built Patons and Baldwins factory. Having established that there was no immediate threat to its ownership of the undertaking, the Council introduced motorbuses on three new routes in April 1950, thus ending the monopoly of electric traction in the town. Following this, a programme of replacing the trolleybus system was commenced, starting with the Harrowgate Hill to Haughton service which last ran on 29th November 1951. At the same time the Harrowgate Hill to Eastbourne service was cut back to the Brougham Street reverser. The remaining routes last operated with trolleybuses on the following dates:-

Brougham Street to Eastbourne (except peak hours) -
                    15th June 1952
Park Lane to Willow Road -
                    6th December 1953
Coniscliffe Road to Cockerton -
                    31st October 1954
Brougham Street to Eastbourne (peak hours) -
                    July 1956
Neasham Road to Faverdale -
                    31st July 1957

The final closure had been delayed for several months due to the Suez oil crisis, and the remaining eight Karrier utility trolleybuses made their final journeys on the last day of July. There was no ceremony, the only public indication of their passing coming from valedictory articles in the local press. One day the trolleys were there and the next day they had gone – a disappointing end to Darlington's electric street transport era.

PRE-ELECTRIC

1   This is a very early view of Darlington town centre showing High Row looking north before the area was terraced at the turn of the century. The Market Hall is on the right behind the horse drawn cabs. In the distance is a single deck horse car at the Prebend Row terminus. The rails in the foreground, turning into Horsemarket, are part of the extension to Bank Top Station via the Market Place, Feethams and Victoria Road which was abandoned in 1885, although it is not known how long the rails remained in place. Following their removal, the rail head was just beyond the Tubwell Row junction in West Row. (Darlington Centre for Local Studies / P Battersby collection)

2   Horse tram no 12, one of the small four-window cars, is seen at the Cockerton terminus on the Darlington side of Cockerton bridge, ready to return to The King's Head. Note the company name on the side of the car, this view dating from before the take-over by the Imperial Tramways Company in 1896. (G.Coates collection)

INSPECTION, OPENING
AND CONVERSION

3   This photograph is believed to have been taken on the occasion of the Board of Trade inspection of the Light Railway system, which took place on 25th May 1904. The highest numbered car, 16, is seen in Freeman's Place, approximately 200 yards from the depot. Note the curtains inside the saloon. (S Lockwood collection)

4   The opening of the Corporation's electric light railway system occurred on Wednesday 1st June 1904. This is the scene on the High Row, looking towards Prebend Row with four cars, led by no 1. The lady at the controls is Mrs A Henderson, wife of the Mayor.
(JS King collection)

←————— 5 Darlington's first trolleybus, appropriately no 1, was delivered on 21st December 1925, making a successful trial run to Haughton on the following day. This photograph, from the Northern Despatch newspaper, shows the vehicle leaving the depot for this first appearance under its own power. The press commented that it 'tootled along merrily'. Public operation commenced at 12.15pm on Sunday 17th January 1926, when two trolleybuses started running on the Haughton route. Although there was no formal opening ceremony, civic leaders did ride on the first public journey and the Mayor was issued with the first ticket. The tram conversion programme was completed on 10th April, when Darlington's official last tram ran that evening to Harrowgate Hill. Again there was no formal ceremony but the Mayor was in attendance and obtained the last tram ticket. Darlingtonians were unsure how to refer to the new 'cars'. The press report of this trial run was headlined 'Darlington's new trams'. The terms 'railless car' and 'trackless' were common for a time, but by the early 1930s the name 'trolleybus' had become the norm. (The Northern Echo)

6　This superb shot of Straker 7 was taken in March 1926 when the trams were still running to Harrowgate Hill. The vehicle is turning from Tubwell Row into West Row whilst operating the Haughton to Market Place shuttle service, before this was extended to Harrowgate Hill in the following month. The overhead tram and trolleybus wiring junction at this point is evident and it is a pity that there is not a tram in view. Note how flimsy the thin wheels of the vehicle look.
(AEI / JS King collection)

7   Once the trolleybuses were established, the tram tracks were gradually removed from the streets. This view of Straker trolleybus 3 approaching Cockerton shows the track, single at this point, in the process of removal. (S.Lockwood collection)

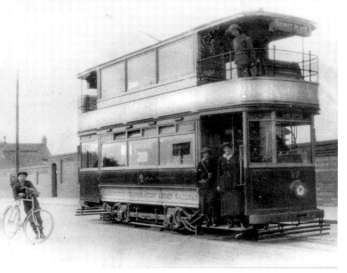

HARROWGATE HILL

8   The route to Harrowgate Hill, 1.8 miles long, was entirely on the Great North Road (A1) heading north out of Darlington. It was the busiest service because it passed the North Road Locomotive Works and was always regarded as the 'main line'. Regular short working cars ran as far as a crossover at St Paul's Church, just beyond the railway works. The terminus at Harrowgate Hill was at the junction of Longfield Road, which in early tramway days was still known under its original name of Honeypot Lane. Services from here ran through the town centre to Eastbourne. Any doubts that the two covered-top double-deck trams could negotiate the North Road railway bridge are dispelled by this view of car 17 at Harrowgate Hill terminus during the First World War. It is only operating as far as the Market Place due to its inability to pass under the station bridges in Parkgate. Parts of the wall in the background, which skirted the waterworks formerly situated here, still exist. (S Lockwood collection)

9   The trolleybus service from Harrowgate Hill comprised two cross-town services, with alternate journeys operating to Eastbourne and Haughton respectively. Trolleybuses turned at Harrowgate Hill by means of a tight turning circle at the junction with Longfield Road at the same point as the tram terminus. Here, Karrier streamliner 11 is in mid-turn shortly after being delivered in 1942. Despite being wartime, the vehicle is in fully lined out livery with the cream relief extending around the rear window. This latter feature was discontinued after the war. The water tower of the Harrowgate Hill waterworks is prominent in this view. (R Marshall collection)

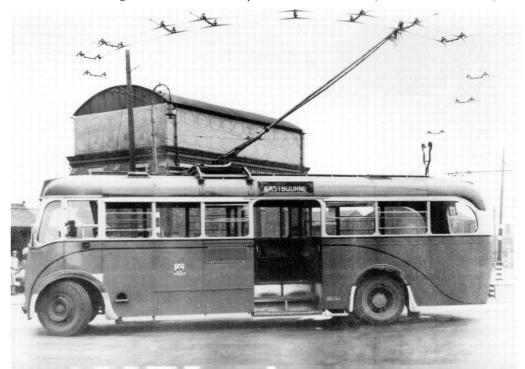

10   This view looking north shows the turning circle. This photograph is one of a series taken just before trolleybus operation ended, during tests to see whether the new longer motorbuses could turn safely at the junction. One of these is seen on the left. When motorbuses took over, they used an alternative routeing to turn, and in 1955 a purpose built turning circle (which still exists), was constructed for them at the north side of the Longfield Road junction. This, of course, was never used by trolleybuses. Trolleybus operation was abandoned in November 1951 and the wiring cut back to the Brougham Street reverser, a distance of 0.65 miles (see next photograph). Note the round '5' speed limit sign hanging from the overhead at the approach to the wiring circle. These were erected in later years at all overhead junctions and circles. (S.Lockwood collection)

11   A reversing triangle for trolleybuses was provided at the entrance to Cumberland Street. Trolleybuses that turned here showed 'Brougham Street', the next street south, on their destination blinds. From November 1951, when motorbuses took over the Harrowgate Hill route, this was the limit of the overhead wiring and the service ran from here to Lingfield Lane and McMullen Road until 1956, although after mid June 1952 the trolleybus service was at peak hours only. In 1952, Leyland streamliner 57 is seen in Cumberland Street with another vehicle of the same type having reversed in front of it. Note the 'McMullen Road Terminus' card in the nearside windscreen.   (R Marshall)

12   The upper part of North Road beyond St Paul's Church was sometimes known as Durham Road. It was not built up on the east side until after tramway operation ceased, as this early 1920s view of ex-Sheerness car 20 shows. The car is passing Zetland Street on its way to the Market Place showing the vista of green fields. In the distance is the locomotive building works of Robert Stephenson and Company at Springfield, known locally as 'Stivvies'. (S.Lockwood collection)

13   The North Road horse tram terminus was at Wales Street, a short distance north of the railway workshops and near St Paul's Church. One of the double deck cars, no 54, is seen at the terminus with North Road Methodist Church in the background. Note the 'Imperial Tramways Company' title over the windows and 'Darlington Tramways' on the rocker panel. (Darlington Centre for Local Studies / P Battersby collection)

←——— 14   The North Eastern Railway / LNER locomotive workshops were situated on North Road, and the main entrance is seen here on the left with no fewer than five Straker trolleybuses in view. North Road Shops, as the workshops were commonly known, provided the main passenger traffic for the Harrowgate Hill route. The works closed in April 1966 and the site was eventually developed as a Morrison's supermarket, making a different type of 'North Road Shops'. The works clock, visible in the centre of this view, has been salvaged and re-erected on the wall of the supermarket in its approximate original position. This commercial postcard, posted in 1928, dates from the earliest days of the trolleybuses, because the tram track is still in evidence. (Commercial Postcard / S. Lockwood collection)

←——— 15 The North Road railway bridge is seen in horse tram days. This structure is dated 1856 and was replaced later in the century by the present bridge shown in the next photo. The bridge caused problems for double-deck cars, and when ex-Sheerness open-top cars were introduced, prominent notices were erected on nearby traction poles warning passengers to remain seated. The double-deck trolleybuses, purchased for this route, were never able to operate on it because of this bridge. The railway over the bridge, originally the Stockton and Darlington Railway main line, is today the branch line to Bishop Auckland and North Road Station, off to the left, is now an un-staffed halt.
(Darlington Centre for Local Studies / P Battersby collection)

16   A 1938 view of High Northgate, near the railway bridge, features Straker 21 on the Eastbourne service. A few yards further south, behind the camera, is the junction with Station Road, where the Willow Road trolleybus service branched off the Harrowgate Hill route.
(G Coates collection)

17   High Northgate, seen here, connects North Road and Northgate. Centre poles were used here, and just in front of the tram in this view is the crossover at Leadenhall Street which was installed to allow extra cars to serve patrons of the Theatre Royal (situated behind the camera). This facility was rarely, if ever used. The first 1860s horse car line ran in the left (west) gutter of Northgate and High Northgate, much to the annoyance of residents who required deliveries of coal. (AD Packer collection)

BARTON STREET AND HAUGHTON

18   Trolleybuses reached the final Haughton terminus in November 1933, when a third of a mile extension was opened from Haughton Green to Haughton Gatehouse, situated at the junction of Stockton Road, Whinfield Road and Barmpton Lane. A turning circle was provided at the road junction. Before making the turn, Leyland 50 stands in Stockton Road. Today, the roads have been re-aligned to the right of this view, and where no 50 is standing is now a cul-de-sac service road. (S.Lockwood collection)

19   A Straker seen in wartime, with masked headlights and white edging paint. No 15 makes the turn at Haughton to proceed to the loading stop. This vehicle was the last Straker to survive, not being withdrawn until the end of 1946. This was probably due to it being used for driver training purposes, for which it was fitted with an additional brake pedal. (AE Old / R Marshall collection)

20   Another wartime view shows English Electric 27 at the terminal stop where a substantial passenger shelter was provided. (AE Old)

21   Until November 1933, the original terminus at Haughton (properly known as Haughton–le–Skerne), was at the Green, where a turning circle was provided opposite the Grey Horse public house. This view, looking towards Haughton Church is of a Straker probably in the first year of the service. When the route was extended along Stockton Road to Haughton Gatehouse, this turning circle was not retained. Unfortunately for us, the publisher of the card has seen fit to erase from the photograph all the overhead wiring and even the trolley gear from the vehicle. (Commercial postcard / Darlington Centre for Local Studies / G Flynn)

22   Originally, the Haughton trolleybus service crossed the Borough boundary at Haughton Bridge, seen here. A clause in the 1925 Act allowed operation up to one mile outside the boundary although in 1930, the date of this photograph, Haughton was incorporated into the Borough. Newly delivered English Electric trolleybuses, led by 29, pose for the camera. Haughton Church can just be seen in the centre-left background above the vehicles, and the road junction with Lingfield Lane is in the right foreground. (English Electric)

HAUGHTON

Approximate times Trolley Buses leave Market Place for Haughton:—

Sundays	Mondays		Tuesdays to Fridays		Saturdays
*10.57 a.m.	*6.37 a.m.	4.12 p.m.	The same as	1.27 p.m.	*6.37 a.m.
*11.7 ,,	*6.47 ,,	4.17 ,,	Mondays	1.37 ,,	*6.47 ,,
*11.17 ,,	*6.57 ,,	4.22 ,,	until		*6.57 ,,
*11.27 ,,	7.7 ,,	4.27 ,,	9.17 a.m.	and every	7.7 ,,
*11.37 ,,	7.17 ,,	4.32 ,,	9.25 ,,	10 minutes	7.17 ,,
*11.47 ,,	7.27 ,,	4.37 ,,	9.35 ,,	until	7.27 ,,
11.57 ,,	and every	4.47 ,,	9.45 ,,	4.57 p.m.	7.37 ,,
	10 minutes	4.57 ,,	9.55 ,,	5.2 ,,	
and every	until	5.2 ,,	and every	5.7 ,,	and every
10 minutes	11.57 a.m.	5.7 ,,	10 minutes	5.12 ,,	10 minutes
until	12.2 p.m.	5.12 ,,	until	5.17 ,,	until
	12.7 ,,	5.17 ,,	11.5 p.m.	5.22 ,,	
10.37 p.m.	12.12 ,,	5.22 ,,	*11.12 ,,	5.27 ,,	10.7 a.m.
10.52 ,,	12.17 ,,	5.27 ,,	11.15 ,,	5.32 ,,	10.12 ,,
	12.22 ,,	5.32 ,,	11.25 ,,	5.37 ,,	10.17 ,,
On Sundays	12.27 ,,	5.37 ,,	11.35 ,,	*5.42 ,,	10.22 ,,
Haughton	12.37 ,,	*5.42 ,,	11.45 ,,	5.47 ,,	10.27 ,,
buses leave	12.42 ,,	5.47 ,,	11.55 ,,	5.57 ,,	10.32 ,,
from Market	12.47 ,,	5.57 ,,	12.2 p.m.	6.7 ,,	10.37 ,,
Hall up to	12.52 ,,	6.7 ,,	12.7 ,,	6.12 ,,	
and including	12.57 ,,	6.12 ,,	12.12 ,,	6.17 ,,	and every
*5.7 p.m.	1.2 ,,	6.17 ,,	12.17 ,,	6.22 ,,	5 minutes
	1.7 ,,	6.22 ,,	12.22 ,,	6.27 ,,	until
	1.17 ,,	6.27 ,,	12.27 ,,	6.37 ,,	
	1.27 ,,	6.37 ,,	12.37 ,,	6.47 ,,	11.22 p.m.
	1.37 ,,	6.47 ,,	12.42 ,,	6.57 ,,	
	and every	6.57 ,,	12.47 ,,		
	10 minutes	and every	12.52 ,,	and every	
	until	10 minutes	12.57 ,,	10 minutes	*From Market
	3.57 p.m.	until	1.2 ,,	until	Hall
	4.2 ,,	11.7 p.m.	1.7 ,,	11.7 p.m.	
	4.7 ,,	11.22 ,,	1.17 ,,	11.22 ,,	

Trolley Buses leave Haughton for Market Place as under:—

Sundays	Mondays		Tuesdays to Fridays		Saturdays
11.12 a.m.	6.42 a.m.	4.12 p.m.	6.42 a.m.	1.17 p.m.	6.42 a.m.
11.22 ,,	6.52 ,,	4.17 ,,	6.52 ,,	1.22 ,,	6.52 ,,
11.32 ,,	7.2 ,,	4.22 ,,	7.2 ,,	1.32 ,,	7.2 ,,
11.42 ,,	7.12 ,,	4.27 ,,	7.12 ,,	1.42 ,,	7.12 ,,
11.52 ,,	7.22 ,,	4.32 ,,	7.22 ,,	1.52 ,,	7.22 ,,
	7.32 ,,	4.37 ,,	7.32 ,,		7.32 ,,
and every	and every	4.42 ,,		and every	
10 minutes	10 minutes	4.47 ,,	and every	10 minutes	and every
until	until	4.52 ,,	10 minutes	until	10 minutes
	8.32 a.m.	5.2 ,,	until		until
10.42 p.m.	8.37 ,,	5.12 ,,	8.32 a.m.	5.12 p.m.	
*10.52 ,,	8.42 ,,	5.17 ,,	8.37 ,,	5.17 ,,	8.42 a.m.
*11.6 ,,	8.47 ,,	5.22 ,,	8.42 ,,	5.22 ,,	8.47 ,,
	8.52 ,,	5.27 ,,	8.47 ,,	5.27 ,,	9.2 ,,
	9.2 ,,	5.32 ,,	8.50 ,,	5.32 ,,	9.12 ,,
	9.12 ,,	5.37 ,,	9.0 ,,	5.37 ,,	9.22 ,,
	and every	5.42 ,,	9.10 ,,	5.42 ,,	9.32 ,,
	10 minutes	5.47 ,,	9.20 ,,	5.47 ,,	
	until	5.52 ,,		5.52 ,,	and everyy
	12.12 p.m.	5.57 ,,	and every	5.57 ,,	10 minutes
	12.17 ,,	6.2 ,,	10 minutes	6.2 ,,	until
	12.22 ,,	6.12 ,,	until	6.12 ,,	
	12.27 ,,	6.22 ,,	11.20 a.m.	6.22 ,,	10.2 a.m.
	12.32 ,,	6.27 ,,	11.27 ,,	6.26 ,,	10.7 ,,
	12.37 ,,	6.32 ,,	11.32 ,,	6.32 ,,	10.12 ,,
	12.42 ,,	6.37 ,,	11.42 ,,	6.37 ,,	10.17 ,,
	12.52 ,,	6.42 ,,	11.52 ,,	6.42 ,,	10.22 ,,
	12.57 ,,	6.52 ,,	12.2 p.m.	6.52 ,,	10.27 ,,
	1.2 ,,	7.2 ,,	12.12 ,,		10.32 ,,
	1.7 ,,	7.12 ,,	12.17 ,,		10.37 ,,
	1.12 ,,	7.22 ,,	12.22 ,,	and every	
	1.17 ,,	and every	12.27 ,,	10 minutes	and every
	1.22 ,,	10 minutes	12.32 ,,	until	5 minutes
	1.32 ,,	until	12.37 ,,		until
	1.42 ,,	10.42 p.m.	12.42 ,,	10.42 p.m.	
	1.52 ,,	10.50 ,,	12.52 ,,	10.50 ,,	*11.27 p.m.
	and every	11.0 ,,	12.57 ,,	11.0 ,,	*11.32 ,,
	10 minutes	11.10 ,,	1.2 ,,	11.10 ,,	*11.35 ,,
	until	*11.20 ,,	1.7 ,,	*11.20 ,,	
		*11.35 ,,	1.12 ,,	*11.35 ,,	*To Depot
					only

Buses due from Haughton Green approx. 1 minute later; from Barton Street approx.
7 minutes later on inward journey.

23   Barton Street tram terminus was situated several yards north of the Haughton Road/Barton Street junction. Car 15 is operating on the shuttle service to the Market Place and is ready to depart. This view dates from just before the First World War. (G Coates collection)

24   Just south of the tram terminus the original Stockton and Darlington Railway crossed Haughton Road by this bridge. In March 1926, only a few weeks after the introduction of trolleybuses to Haughton, Straker no 1 stands by the bridge and in the distance no 7 'tootles along' towards Haughton passing the former tram terminus. The railway survived until 1967 after which the bridge was removed. Since 1887 it had been a freight only line, apart from the occasional diversion of passenger trains due to engineering work. (AEI / Stanley King collection)

25   Turning 180 degrees from the previous photograph, this 1930 view shows Haughton Road rising up to cross the east coast main line railway, before descending towards the depot and the town centre. Newly delivered English Electric trolleybus 32 is in the foreground on a test run. Note how the tramway overhead has been adapted for trolleybuses, with the result that the vehicle's booms have to stretch to reach the wires. The Leyland Titan double-decker bus was owned by United Automobile Services. By the end of 1934, an agreement had been reached between the Corporation and United whereby that company would charge a protective fare of 1/2d above the trolleybus fares on any common routes within the Borough. In return the Corporation would not object to any routes that United wished to introduce. Opposite the United bus, on the left hand side of the road, is Vicarage Road which leads to the Corporation's Hundens highways yard. During the Second World War, the older trolleybuses were dispersed here and wiring was erected to enable this, although details of the layout have not survived. (English Electric)

McMullen Road and a tale of wartime heroism
Although peripheral to the Darlington trolleybus story, readers may be interested to know why Lingfield Lane does not appear on present-day maps of the town. On January 13th 1945, a Lancaster bomber, returning from a routine test flight to its base at RAF Middleton St George, just outside Darlington, developed engine problems. The crew, from a Royal Canadian Air Force squadron, was commanded by Pilot Officer WS McMullen. Despite desperate efforts, it became obvious that the plane could not reach its base and all the crew, apart from McMullen, baled out. He stayed with the aircraft to ensure that it was kept airborne until it had cleared the populated part of Darlington. It crashed in farmland near Lingfield Lane, about 600 yards clear of the nearest housing. McMullen lost his life. Lingfield Lane, which ran between Yarm Road trolleybus terminus and Haughton Road (crossing the original Stockton and Darlington Railway on the level en route), was re-named McMullen Road in honour of the pilot who had undoubtedly saved the lives of many local people by his selfless action.

EASTBOURNE

26   On conversion from trams in 1926, the Eastbourne trolleybuses were initially extended to Geneva Road, and subsequently as far as the Lingfield Lane roundabout in 1942. A final route extension, the last in Darlington, opened in March 1949 when a half mile route of wiring was opened along McMullen Road to the gates of the large Patons and Baldwins factory complex built after the war. The company paid half the cost of the overhead installation and Eastbourne trolleybuses operated to here at shift times until the final abandonment of the route in 1956. Because vehicles could not show 'McMullen Road' on their screens, a large card was shown in the windscreen when working to this point. The terminus was at a turning circle in a lay-by with shelters. Views of trolleybuses on this section have proved impossible to source, but this less than perfect photograph of McMullen Road looking north, shows the partly erected overhead wiring. On the left can be seen the temporary housing provided during the Second World War for workers engaged in ordnance production. (Darlington Centre for Local Studies)

27   From 9th December 1942, the half mile extension from Geneva Road to a new terminus at the junction with Lingfield Lane was brought into operation. Trolleybuses turned by means of the roundabout here. After the extension along McMullen Road was opened in 1949, the main trolleybus service continued to terminate at 'Lingfield Lane', with the extended journeys only operating at peak hours and shift times. However, from June 1952, the entire Eastbourne service ran at peak hours only, the basic service being motorbus operated. This situation lasted until the end of July 1956, when the entry into service of a batch of new buses resulted in the trolleybuses being finally withdrawn from the route. This view, taken about 1950, shows Karrier Utility 24 standing at the terminal stop at the southwest part of the roundabout. This trolleybuses later ran in single-deck form in Bradford.   (H Luff/Online Transport Archive/ Photobus)

28   The original Eastbourne trolleybus terminus was at the junction with Geneva Road, where a turning circle was provided at the wide junction. This was a short distance (0.18 miles) beyond the former tram terminus at Cobden Street. The route was always operated as a through service to Harrowgate Hill, as the trams had done, although for the first two years of operation, the Faverdale through service also operated to here until it was diverted to Neasham Road in 1928. Following the further extension of the route to Lingfield Lane in 1942, the circle here was retained and used with lessening frequency until the abandonment of the route. This 1953 view is of Karrier utility 18 standing outside no 230 Yarm Road having just turned on the circle, with Geneva Road in the background. Today, this is an extremely busy junction controlled by traffic lights and it would be inconceivable to have vehicles making a 'U' turn as trolleybuses used to do. (JC Gillham)

CONISCLIFFE ROAD

46   The Coniscliffe Road service ran along the road from Darlington towards Barnard Castle (A67) for a distance of 1.6 miles terminating at the junction with Baydale Road, where there was a tight turning circle. To assist vehicles turning here, the kerb line opposite the junction was cut back, as seen in this view of Karrier streamliner 1 making the turn. Despite being almost fifty years since trolleybuses ran here, this kerb line has been faithfully maintained and can still be seen today. The terminus within walking distance of the River Tees, and the service was popular on fine weekends transporting trippers visiting the riverbank. On such busy occasions, the double-deck trolleybuses were sometimes pressed in service to operate additional journeys on this route. After the war, a turning point using a triangular reverser was proposed at the junction with Woodburn Drive (opposite Salutation Road junction). The site of this was inspected by the Ministry of Transport but nothing came of the proposals. (S.Lockwood collection)

CONISCLIFFE ROAD.

Approximate times Trolley Buses leave Market Place for Con"iscliffe Road:—

Sundays	Mondays		Tuesdays to Fridays		Saturdays	
*11.0 a.m.	*6.50 a.m.	*11.17 a.m.	The same as	4.12 p.m.	*6.50 a.m.	and every
*11.10 ,,	*7.0 ,,	11.20 ,,	Mondays	*4.17 ,,	*7.0 ,,	5 minutes
11.20 ,,	7.10 ,,	11.27 ,,	until	4.22 ,,	7.10 ,,	until
11.30 ,,	7.20 ,,	11.30 ,,		4.27 ,,	7.20 ,,	
11.40 ,,	*7.27 ,,	11.37 ,,	11.0 a.m.	4.32 ,,	7.30 ,,	9.2 p.m.
11.50 ,,	7.30 ,,	11.40 ,,	11.10 ,,	4.37 ,,	7.40 ,,	9.12 ,,
	7.40 ,,	11.47 ,,	11.20 ,,		7.50 ,,	
and every	7.50 ,,	11.52 ,,	*11.27 ,,	and every	8.0 ,,	and every
10 minutes	8.0 ,,	11.57 ,,	11.30 ,,	5 minutes	8.10 ,,	10 minutes
until	8.7 ,,	12.2 p.m.	*11.37 ,,	until	8.15 ,,	until
	8.12 ,,	12.7 ,,	11.40 ,,		8.20 ,,	
1.50 p.m.	*8.17 ,,	12.12 ,,	*11.47 ,,	7.12 p.m.	8.30 ,,	11.22 p.m.
*1.57 ,,	8.22 ,,	12.17 ,,	11.50 ,,	7.22 ,,	8.35 ,,	
2.0 ,,	8.27 ,,	12.22 ,,	11.57 ,,	7.32 ,,	8.40 ,,	
*2.7 ,,	8.32 ,,		12.0 noon		8.45 ,,	
2.10 ,,	8.37 ,,	and every	12.7 p.m.	and every	8.50 ,,	
2.17 ,,	8.42 ,,	5 minutes	12.12 ,,	10 minutes	9.0 ,,	
2.20 ,,	8.47 ,,	until	12.17 ,,	until	9.10 ,,	
2.27 ,,	8.57 ,,		12.22 ,,		9.20 ,,	
2.30 ,,	9.7 ,,	7.52 p.m.	12.27 ,,	11.22 p.m.	9.30 ,,	
2.37 ,,	9.12 ,,	8.2 ,,			9.40 ,,	*Start from
2.42 ,,	9.20 ,,	8.12 ,,	and every		9.50 ,,	Market Hall
2.47 ,,	9.30 ,,	8.22 ,,	5 minutes		*9.57 ,,	
2.52 ,,			until		10.0 ,,	
2.57 ,,	and every	and every			*10.7 ,,	
	10 minutes	10 minutes	2.12 p.m.		10.10 ,,	
and every	until	until	2.22 ,,		10.17 ,,	
5 minutes			2.32 ,,		10.22 ,,	
until	11.0 a.m.	11.22 p.m.			10.27 ,,	
10.42 p.m.	*11.7 ,,		and every		10.32 ,,	
10.52 ,,	11.10 ,,		10 minutes			
			until			

Approximate times Trolley Buses leave Coniscliffe Road for Market Place:—

Sundays	Mondays		Tuesdays to Fridays		Saturdays	
11.11 a.m.	7.1 a.m.	11.11 a.m.	The same as	4.38 p.m.	7.1 a.m.	10.1 a.m.
11.21 ,,	7.11 ,,	11.18 ,,	Monday	4.43 ,,	7.11 ,,	10.8 ,,
11.31 ,,	7.21 ,,	11.23 ,,	until	4.48 ,,	7.21 ,,	10.13 ,,
11.41 ,,	7.31 ,,	11.28 ,,			7.31 ,,	10.18 ,,
11.51 ,,	7.38 ,,	11.33 ,,	11.11 a.m.	and every	7.41 ,,	10.23 ,,
	7.43 ,,	11.38 ,,	11.21 ,,	5 minutes		10.28 ,,
and every	7.53 ,,		11.31 ,,	until	and every	10.33 ,,
10 minutes	8.3 ,,	and every	11.38 ,,		10 minutes	
until	8.13 ,,	5 minutes	11.43 ,,		until	and every
	8.18 ,,	until	11.48 ,,	7.23 p.m.		5 minutes
2.1 p.m.	8.23 ,,		11.53 ,,	7.33 ,,	8.21 a.m.	until
2.8 ,,	and every	7.58 p.m.	11.58 ,,	7.43 ,,	8.26 ,,	
2.13 ,,	5 minutes	8.3 ,,		7.53 ,,	8.31 ,,	9.13 p.m.
2.18 ,,	until	8.13 ,,	and every		8.41 ,,	9.23 ,,
2.23 ,,		8.23 ,,	5 minutes	and every	8.46 ,,	9.33 ,,
2.28 ,,	8.43 a.m.	8.33 ,,	until	10 minutes	8.51 ,,	
2.33 ,,	8.51 ,,			until	8.56 ,,	and every
	8.53 ,,	and every	2.23 p.m.		9.1 ,,	10 minutes
and every	9.1 ,,	10 minutes	2.33 ,,	11.33 p.m.	9.11 ,,	until
5 minutes	9.11 ,,	until	2.43 ,,		9.21 ,,	
until	9.21 ,,		2.53 ,,		9.31 ,,	11.33 p.m.
	9.31 ,,	11.33 p.m.			9.41 ,,	
11.3 p.m.	9.41 ,,		and every			
			10 minutes		and every	
	and every		until		10 minutes	
	10 minutes				until	
	until		4.23 p.m.			
			4.28 ,,			
			4.33 ,,			

Buses due from junction of Carmel Road and Coniscliffe Road approx. 3 minutes later on inward journey.

47   Karrier utility 10 stands at the Coniscliffe Road terminal stop on 7th March 1953. The style of housing at the terminus was typical of that all along this suburban route. Note the time clock, which was a feature of Darlington's termini. This was to ensure that the correct departure time was observed, the conductor having to insert a card into the mechanism which punched the time on to the card. From December 1953, when the Willow Road circular was abandoned, the route would operate only to Cockerton until the Coniscliffe Road route itself closed in October 1954. (D.Williams)

48   Close to the town centre, Coniscliffe Road narrowed near the junction with Cleveland Terrace. Here these 19th century cottages at Mount Pleasant were demolished in the 1960s and replaced by modern flats. Leyland streamliner 63, on a journey from Coniscliffe Road to Willow Road just after the war, shows the immediate post-war livery with the rear of the vehicle showing two tones of blue. This view seems to emphasise the length of the trolley booms required on single deck trolleybuses. (Darlington Centre for Local Studies)